US MILITARY

DELTA FORCE

BY CHARLES MARLIN

WWW.APEXEDITIONS.COM

Apex is distributed by North Star Editions:
sales@northstareditions.com | 888-417-0195

Produced for Apex by Red Line Editorial.

Photographs ©: US Army/Alamy, cover; Courtney Bacon/DVIDS, 1, 6–7; SOF AT&L/DVIDS, 4–5; Brennan Linsley/AP Images, 8–9; AP Images, 10–11; Bettmann/Getty Images, 12; Steven D. Starr/Corbis Historical/Getty Images, 13; Chris Hondros/Getty Images News/Getty Images, 14–15; Sgt. Monique O'Neill/DVIDS, 16–17; Shutterstock Images, 18, 19, 22–23, 24–25, 29; Greg Mathieson/Mai/The Chronicle Collection/Getty Images, 20–21; Spc. Giovanny Lopez/US Army/DVIDS, 24; Petty Officer 1st Class Elisandro T. Diaz/US Navy/DVIDS, 27

Library of Congress Control Number: 2025939213

ISBN
979-8-89250-804-9 (hardcover)
979-8-89250-833-9 (paperback)
979-8-89250-888-9 (ebook pdf)
979-8-89250-862-9 (hosted ebook)

Printed in the United States of America
Mankato, MN
012026

NOTE TO PARENTS AND EDUCATORS

Apex books are designed to build literacy skills in striving readers. Exciting, high-interest content attracts and holds readers' attention. The text is carefully leveled to allow students to achieve success quickly. Additional features, such as bolded glossary words for difficult terms, help build comprehension.

TABLE OF CONTENTS

CHAPTER 1

SNEAK ATTACK

A helicopter lands near an enemy building. A US Army Delta Force team jumps out. The soldiers enter the building and begin to search. An enemy leader is somewhere inside.

MH-6 Little Birds are small helicopters. Delta Force teams often use them.

It's pitch-black in the building. So, the soldiers use their night vision goggles. They break down doors to check each room.

Night vision goggles can attach to a soldier's helmet.

FAST FACT

Delta Force sometimes uses door charges. These bombs can break down doors.

Most rooms are empty. But one has the enemy leader hiding inside. The soldiers put him in handcuffs. They take him back to their helicopter.

SUPER SECRET

Many Delta Force **missions** involve sneakiness and surprise. So, the missions are classified. The public doesn't know about most of them.

Some of the people that Delta Force catches end up in high-security prisons.

CHAPTER 2

DELTA FORCE HISTORY

In the 1970s, a US colonel worked with a British **special ops** team. The team did tough and secretive missions. The colonel thought the US Army needed a similar team.

Delta Force was founded by Colonel Charles Beckwith (center).

Panama's leader committed many crimes in the 1980s. Delta Force helped get him to turn himself in.

Delta Force formed in 1977. The team often took down dangerous people. It also spied on enemies. Sometimes, it worked to rescue people.

RESCUE AND ATTACK

In 1989, Panama's **dictator** sent an American man to prison. Delta Force rescued the man. Then the team helped the US Army take down the dictator.

Thousands of US troops went to fight in Panama in 1989 and 1990.

In the 2000s, Delta Force carried out many missions in the Middle East. The team often fought against **terrorists**.

FAST FACT

Delta Force is sometimes called "The Unit."

In 2003, Delta Force helped find the hiding spot of Saddam Hussein. He was the dictator of Iraq.

CHAPTER 3

TESTS AND TRAINING

Soldiers join Delta Force after serving in other parts of the US Army. They must pass a month-long course. It includes tough workouts and long hikes. Soldiers also practice **navigation**.

Many soldiers join Delta Force after being Green Berets (pictured) or Army Rangers.

Some Delta Force tests take place at Fort Bragg in North Carolina.

Tests check soldiers' strength and speed. Soldiers also get asked tough questions. Military leaders pick which soldiers can join Delta Force.

"THE LONG WALK"

One physical test is called "The Long Walk." Soldiers must carry a 45-pound (20-kg) rucksack. They lug it on a 40-mile (64-km) march.

Soldiers often use large bags called rucksacks to hold their gear.

If selected, soldiers do six months of training. They practice fighting, spying, and using **explosives**. Soldiers also practice working together as a team.

FAST FACT

When training, soldiers have practice missions. They act out what they would do to fight enemies.

Delta Force soldiers learn to jump from aircraft using parachutes.

CHAPTER 4

HIGH-RISK MISSIONS

Delta Force includes about 2,000 soldiers. They are divided into groups called squadrons. Each squadron carries out missions. One squadron focuses on hacking. Another does spy work.

Some soldiers hack into enemy computer systems.
They may try to get secret information.

Delta Force missions are risky. So, soldiers carry many weapons. They often use **assault rifles**. They may wear body armor, too.

Some soldiers use grenade launchers. These weapons shoot small bombs called grenades.

Many Delta Force soldiers carry HK416 assault rifles.

FAST FACT

Delta Force often uses armored vehicles. These large trucks have hard plates on their outsides.

Delta Force often carries out short, quick attacks. These are called direct action missions. Delta Force may also help other special ops teams complete missions.

DARING RESCUE

In 2012, terrorists in Libya attacked a US **diplomatic** building. Delta Force soldiers flew there with other special ops teams. They helped fight back. And they rescued American workers.

The Night Stalkers are another special ops team in the US Army. They often do nighttime attacks.

COMPREHENSION QUESTIONS

Write your answers on a separate piece of paper.

1. Write a few sentences explaining the main ideas of Chapter 3.
2. What part of Delta Force training do you think would be the hardest? Why?
3. When was Delta Force founded?
   - A. 1977
   - B. 1989
   - C. 2003
4. Why might Delta Force keep its missions secret?
   - A. so the public doesn't try to join Delta Force
   - B. so enemies don't know the team's plans
   - C. so enemies don't help Delta Force

5. What does **classified** mean in this book?

*So, the missions are **classified**. The public doesn't know about most of them.*

- **A.** very famous
- **B.** kept secret
- **C.** not true

6. What does **physical** mean in this book?

*One **physical** test is called "The Long Walk." Soldiers must carry a 45-pound (20-kg) rucksack.*

- **A.** needing a person's help
- **B.** knowing a person's feelings
- **C.** involving a person's body

Answer key on page 32.

GLOSSARY

assault rifles

Guns that quickly fire many rounds and use parts called magazines to hold ammo.

dictator

A leader with total power, especially one who is cruel.

diplomatic

Involving government workers who live and work in other countries.

explosives

Devices that can blow up, such as bombs.

missions

Tasks or plans with specific goals.

navigation

The process of finding one's location and planning which way to go.

special ops

Military groups or missions requiring extra skills and training.

terrorists

People who attack and scare others to reach their goals.

TO LEARN MORE

BOOKS

Banks, Anita. *US Army*. Apex Editions, 2023.

Hamilton, John. *United States Army*. Abdo Publishing, 2021.

Marlin, Charles. *Helicopters*. Apex Editions, 2025.

ONLINE RESOURCES

Visit **www.apexeditions.com** to find links and resources related to this title.

ABOUT THE AUTHOR

Charles Marlin is an author, editor, and avid cyclist. He lives in rural Iowa.

INDEX

ANSWER KEY:
1. Answers will vary; 2. Answers will vary; 3. A; 4. B; 5. B; 6. C